A scene from the Magic Theatre production of "The House of Yes." Set design by Jeff

Photo by Jeff Rowlings

THE
HOUSE
OF YES

BY WENDY MacLEOD

★

DRAMATISTS
PLAY SERVICE
INC.

THE HOUSE OF YES
Copyright © 1996, Wendy MacLeod

All Rights Reserved

For my teachers,
Lee Breuer and Leon Katz,
who told me to take off the white gloves

THE HOUSE OF YES was produced by SoHo Repertory Theater (Julian Webber, Artistic Director; Chris Kelly, Managing Director) in New York City, in January, 1995. It was directed by Julian Webber; the set design was by Sarah Lambert; the costume design was by James Sauli; the lighting design was by Joe Saint and the sound design was by John Kilgore. The cast was as follows:

MRS. PASCAL	Allison Janney
JACKIE-O	Jodie Markell
ANTHONY	Neal Huff
MARTY	Chris Eigeman
LESLY	Kim Soden

THE HOUSE OF YES was produced by The Gate Theatre in London, England, on March 31, 1993. It was directed by Ian Rickson; the set design was by Lucy Hall; the lighting design was by Tim Mitchell; the composer was Stephen Warbeck; the production manager was Guiseppe di Iorio and the stage managers were Lisa Ellenbogen and Jamie MacDow. The cast was as follows:

MRS. PASCAL	Mary EllenRay
JACKIE-O	Deirdre Harrison
ANTHONY	Matt Bardock
MARTY	Jason Watkins
LESLY	Dena Davis

THE HOUSE OF YES was produced by the Magic Theatre (John Lion, Artistic Director) in San Francisco, California, in April, 1990. It was directed by Andrew Doe; the set design was by Jeff Rowlings; the costume design was by Callie Floor and the lighting design was by Maurice Vercoutere. The cast was as follows:

MRS. PASCAL	Nancy Shelby
JACKIE-O	Celia Shuman
ANTHONY	Kenneth R. Merckx, Jr.
MARTY	Art Manke
LESLY	Amy Resnick

AUTHOR'S NOTES

The play started with a particular house, a house I saw in an elegant suburb of Washington, D.C. There was just something about this chic, moneyed house that made me want in. And Lesly begins the play wanting in.

The title came from graffiti I saw written on a bathroom wall: "We are living in a house of yes." And that made me think about Edgar Allan Poe and pornography and mostly about amorality. The play is about people that have never been said no to. It's about an insularity I see in the upper classes, people who have cut themselves off from the rest of the world and are living by the rules they've invented.

It is a great mistake to imagine the play is "camp" because the characters pretend to be Jack and Jackie Kennedy. To do the play that way is to undermine its emotional truth, and the love, however twisted, between the characters. Mrs. Pascal desperately loves her daughter and is trying to protect her, and the twins love each other deeply, tragically. However to speak of such things is "déclassé" and the characters only allow themselves that luxury at one or two points in the play. It is that tension between the Noel Coward veneer and the Pinteresque subtext that makes the play both funny and moving.

Some common questions. What's the deal with Anthony? Why does he do what he does? Perhaps because he truly loves Lesly and shares his brother's longing for "normalcy." Perhaps he's out to finally outdo his older brother. Or perhaps he tears Marty and Lesly apart for his sister's sake.

What's the deal with the assassination game? The construct of the two Kennedys allows the twins to make love to each other. In a blurring of events, they have confused the Kennedys with their own parents and we are merely watching an X-rated version of children playing house.

Finally, who is telling the truth at the end of the play? Did Mr. Pascal walk out on the family or was he, in fact, murdered by Mrs. Pascal? I will only say that every actor must present their character's version with absolute conviction.

Wendy MacLeod
August 1995

CAST OF CHARACTERS

JACKIE-O
MARTY, Jackie-O's twin brother
ANTHONY, their younger brother
MRS. PASCAL, their mother
LESLY, Marty's fiancee

SETTING

McLean, Virginia, a wealthy suburb of Washington, D.C., around the corner from the Kennedys.

The living room, and a guest bedroom, in the Pascals' house.

TIME

Thanksgiving, during a hurricane, some 20 years after JFK's assassination.

NOTE: The walls of the living room would be covered with paintings but we don't see paintings, only frames which suggest the walls. The low, black leather sofa is actually a chic simulation of a car seat, perhaps the back seat of a limousine. The floors are black-and-white-checked linoleum. Select objects suggest the family has lived abroad — a camel saddle hassock, an Italian triptych, etc.

The characters shouldn't enter and exit, they should appear and disappear, suggesting that spies are everywhere.

The "game" should probably be underscored with music, to heighten the ritual.

THE HOUSE OF YES
(A Suburban Jacobean Play)

Scene 1

Sound of hurricane. Lights up on Jackie-O furiously rearranging the furniture. Anthony enters and watches her. Long pause.

ANTHONY. It looked better before. *(Jackie-O ignores him.)* It's all getting blown away anyway. You gonna move the TV?

JACKIE-O. Too many wires.

ANTHONY. Good. I want to watch the football game.

JACKIE-O. What football game?

ANTHONY. Any football game.

JACKIE-O. Help me move this coffee table.

ANTHONY. Move it where?

JACKIE-O. In front of the sofa.

ANTHONY. That's no good.

JACKIE-O. That's where coffee tables go. In front of sofas. Help me masking tape the windows.

ANTHONY. You gonna put those crosses?

JACKIE-O. Yeah.

ANTHONY. *(Looking out the window.)* The Kennedys aren't putting crosses on their windows.

JACKIE-O. They could really care. They have ten other houses.

ANTHONY. It's like wearing garlic those crosses.

JACKIE-O. It was on the news. It can't hurt.

ANTHONY. Yes it can. It goos up the windows.

JACKIE-O. Did Marty call?

ANTHONY. Last night.

JACKIE-O. I know last night. Did Marty call today?

ANTHONY. He's bringing a friend.

JACKIE-O. What?

ANTHONY. He said he's bringing a friend.

JACKIE-O. Male or female?

ANTHONY. I don't know.

JACKIE-O. What did he say exactly?

ANTHONY. He said, "Tell Mom I'm bringing a friend."

JACKIE-O. Why not me? Why not, "Tell Jackie I'm bringing a friend?"

ANTHONY. Groceries.

JACKIE-O. What?

ANTHONY. I think it pertained to groceries, bedrooms, like that. Logistics.

JACKIE-O. What else did Marty say?

ANTHONY. He said, "Hello Anthony?" I said, "Yeah. Marty?" He said, "Yeah." We said, *"Hey."*

JACKIE-O. Marty said "hey?"

ANTHONY. Not like hey, like H-E-Y, but like a noise, a noise of jubilation.

JACKIE-O. Marty was jubilant?

ANTHONY. At that point in the phone call. Or at least he was doing a fair impersonation of jubilant.

JACKIE-O. Marty was pretending to be jubilant?

ANTHONY. Oh my God. What's wrong with Marty?

JACKIE-O. And who's this friend?

ANTHONY. And who's this friend? Exactly.

JACKIE-O. Then what did he say?

ANTHONY. He said, "How you doing?" I said, "Good. How *you* doing?" He said, "Good."

JACKIE-O. But he was lying. He's not good. He hates New York. He's coming home.

ANTHONY. For Thanksgiving.

JACKIE-O. For good.

ANTHONY. Did he say that?

JACKIE-O. I don't know. Did he?

ANTHONY. No.

JACKIE-O. How come nobody told me about this friend?
(Mrs. Pascal enters carrying a cocktail.)

MRS. PASCAL.   Jackie, did I tell you your brother's bringing a friend?

JACKIE-O.   What kind of friend?

MRS. PASCAL.   I don't know. Marty's never had a friend before. Who taped up the windows?

JACKIE-O.   I did. I saw it on the news.

MRS. PASCAL.   That tape leaves goo. It goos up the windows.

JACKIE-O.   Goo is what tape is all about. Goo is what makes it tape instead of paper.

MRS. PASCAL.   A person offers a little constructive criticism and a person gets lectured on the nature of things. I came in to ask a question but I can't think what it is. Ah, Anthony, did I make up the guest room?

ANTHONY.   How should I know?

MRS. PASCAL.   A person asks a civilized question and a person gets thrown to the lions. I'll go up and check. *(She turns and looks at the TV.)* Is this a bowl?

ANTHONY.   Yes.

MRS. PASCAL.   Is it a bowl relevant to us in any way?

ANTHONY.   No.

MRS. PASCAL.   Then turn it off. I don't want electrical things on. Anthony, did you give your sister her medication?

ANTHONY.   Uh-huh.

MRS. PASCAL.   Did you check under her tongue? *(Mrs. Pascal exits.)*

ANTHONY.   Were you excited when I came home?

JACKIE-O.   That was different. You were dropping out of college.

ANTHONY.   A *good* college.

JACKIE-O.   So why did you leave?

ANTHONY.   With Marty gone, who was gonna take care of you?

JACKIE-O.   Mama.

ANTHONY.   Yeah. Right.

JACKIE-O.   I hear his car. I hear Marty's car.

ANTHONY.   You can't hear cars. There's a hurricane.

JACKIE-O.   Where's my brush? I had a hairbrush right here.

ANTHONY.   What did it look like?

JACKIE-O. It looked like a hairbrush! Like a brush you brush your hair with!

MRS. PASCAL. *(Re-entering.)* Was it pink?

JACKIE-O. Yes it was pink goddamnit it was pink. It was pink and now it's gone!

MRS. PASCAL. I put it upstairs. I didn't want it around the food.

JACKIE-O. It wasn't around the food. The food is in the kitchen.

MRS. PASCAL. It was on the same floor as the food.

ANTHONY. I have a comb.

JACKIE-O. I don't want a comb! I want a brush! Combs just straighten your hair out, I want it to gleam.

ANTHONY. It is gleaming.

JACKIE-O. It is not!

ANTHONY. It is, it is. I need sunglasses almost.

JACKIE-O. It is?

ANTHONY. It *is. (A wind blows into the house as Marty and Lesly enter, bedraggled, and wet. Jackie-O sees only Marty. She runs to him and straddles her legs around him.)*

JACKIE-O. Marty!

MARTY. Jackie. *(Jackie-O slides off of Marty as she becomes aware of Lesly.)* Lesly. This is Jackie-O. My mother. Anthony. Meet Lesly. Lesly and I are engaged. *(Jackie-O screams then begins to laugh. Every one nervously joins in. Jackie-O stops laughing.)*

JACKIE-O. I have to find my hairbrush.

LESLY. I have a comb. *(Jackie-O just looks at her, then exits.)*

MRS. PASCAL. Marty you're a wreck.

MARTY. I was in a hurricane. I just came in from a hurricane.

MRS. PASCAL. Marty you look thin. Are you thin? You look so thin. Oh my God, I sounded like a mother. Didn't I sound just like a mother?

MARTY. You are a mother.

MRS. PASCAL. I know and I still can't believe it. I look at you people and wonder however did you fit in my womb. Now Marty there's some Liebfraumilch in the kitchen. Why don't you go and pour us a nice glass of Liebfraumilch. Anthony

12

you go too. You can smell the cork or something.

ANTHONY. Can't I stay here?

MRS. PASCAL. No you cannot. This is girl talk in here.

ANTHONY. I like girl talk.

MRS. PASCAL. Well if you were here it wouldn't be girl talk, would it?

ANTHONY. Do I have to smell the cork?

MRS. PASCAL. No darling. You just have to do something in some other location. *(Anthony and Marty exit.)*

LESLY. You have a lovely home.

MRS. PASCAL. Home?

LESLY. Your house. It's lovely.

MRS. PASCAL. Oh yes it was. I mean it is. I mean it will be until it gets blown away. We'll all get blown away to Oz or something.

LESLY. That was a tornado.

MRS. PASCAL. What?

LESLY. A tornado. In *Wizard of Oz.* Not a hurricane.

MRS. PASCAL. Really? Are you sure? *(Lesly nods.)* My. How long have you known Marty?

LESLY. About six months.

MRS. PASCAL. And you know him pretty well, do you?

LESLY. I don't know. I think so. I guess you've met a lot of Marty's girlfriends.

MRS. PASCAL. Not really.

LESLY. I hope I'm the first fiancee.

MRS. PASCAL. You're definitely the first, the very first. And I hope the last.

LESLY. Me too.

MRS. PASCAL. I had one great passion in my life and do you know who that was?

LESLY. Your husband?

MRS. PASCAL. My husband. Precisely. I didn't know he was my one great passion until he was gone. Until he was gone my one great passion was the man I met that night at a party. My one great passion was any man I met that night at a party who could use a new adjective to describe me. I have no idea who my children belong to. All I know for sure is that Jackie

13

and Marty belong to each other. Jackie's hand was holding Marty's penis when they came out of the womb. The doctors swore to me. It's in some medical journal somewhere. *(Pause.)*

LESLY.   Well, I guess I'll go freshen up now.

MRS. PASCAL.   Do. By all means. You're drenched. *(To Anthony, offstage.)* Anthony, did I put clean towels out on the bed?

ANTHONY.   *(Entering.)* How should I know?

MRS. PASCAL.   Go and see. And show Lesly to her room. And show her how to jiggle the toilet so it doesn't run. *(Anthony and Lesly exit. Marty enters with a tray of wine glasses.)* Marty. A word.

MARTY.   A word, Mama, or many words?

MRS. PASCAL.   Now don't get snippy Marty, you've been in this house exactly 37 seconds and you're already snippy. It's no wonder your father died young, he'd simply had it with all the snippiness, a person can die a slow death from being snipped at year after year, the way he said *solid* when meant *salad,* the two of you would not let it go, like a puppy with a rag doll. Or the time he missed the exit on 495, those things *happen* on interstates, mistakes are made, that's what those No U-Turn places are for …

MARTY.   Daddy didn't die a slow death.

MRS. PASCAL.   Let's stick to the subject.

MARTY.   I have no idea what the subject is.

MRS. PASCAL.   I'll tell you what the subject is *not* …

MARTY.   No Mama, that's too broad a category. Tell me what the subject *is.*

MRS. PASCAL.   You. A fiancee. Here. Why?

MARTY.   I love her and I'm trying to follow procedure.

MRS. PASCAL.   Do you love her for any particular reason?

MARTY.   Why? You didn't like her?

MRS. PASCAL.   I talked to her for exactly 37 seconds, Marty. Who is she? What does she do?

MARTY.   She's a waitress in the Donut King on 14th Street. She smells like powdered sugar.

MRS. PASCAL.   Men don't marry girls who smell like powdered sugar. They have a sweet little affair with them which they recall fondly in their twilight years.

14

MARTY. Don't be such a snob.

MRS. PASCAL. Your sister has been out of the hospital less than six months. Last week she nearly lost it because the seltzer water was flat and you bring a woman home. Not just a woman, a fiancee, an anti-Jackie. Are you trying to push your sister over the edge?

MARTY. No.

MRS. PASCAL. Just what then are you trying to do?

MARTY. Be normal.

MRS. PASCAL. Well it's a little late for that, young man.

MARTY. Do you want us to leave?

MRS. PASCAL. Yes I want you to leave, at once, without further ado. As soon as the storm lets up. If you don't, I'll take away your sheets, your towels, everything .

MARTY. What do I tell Lesly?

MRS. PASCAL. Tell her the truth.

MARTY. The truth?

MRS. PASCAL. That your sister's insane. She'll understand.

MARTY. Don't say insane. She's … ill.

MRS. PASCAL. If she were ill, I could give her an aspirin and put her to bed. I could make her that soup you're supposed to make.

MARTY. Chicken noodle.

MRS. PASCAL. That. Alas, I cannot. I mean, I can make the soup for heaven's sake, it comes in a can, but I cannot make her well. I have tried but to no avail.

MARTY. "To no avail." What was that?

MRS. PASCAL. I'm getting dramatic.

MARTY. Well stop it. I thought it was better that I come and tell her myself.

MRS. PASCAL. It would be better if you didn't tell her at all, it would be better if there was nothing to tell, if there is anyone present who knows why this marriage should not take place it is me.

MARTY. Why?

MRS. PASCAL. Why what?

MARTY. Why shouldn't the marriage take place?

MRS. PASCAL. You know why.

MARTY. Tell me. *(Pause.)*
MRS. PASCAL. Excuse me. I'm going to go baste the turkey and hide the sharp objects. *(She exits.)*

CROSSFADE

Scene 2

The guest bedroom.

ANTHONY. So these are the towels. Do you like them 'cause I could get you others. We have black ones with Roman scenes on them.
LESLY. That's okay. These are dry, that's the only thing. *(Pointing to her wet clothes.)* This is just from the car to the door, can you believe it?
ANTHONY. Yes.
LESLY. It's a hurricane.
ANTHONY. I know.
LESLY. I curled my hair this morning. With a curling iron. And now look.
ANTHONY. I always thought a curling iron was shaped like an iron.
LESLY. No. It's like a hot dog.
ANTHONY. I know.
LESLY. *(Looking into the mirror.)* This is 'sposed to be waterproof mascara. Ha ha.
ANTHONY. You look lovely. Did I show you the toilet thing?
LESLY. Yeah.
ANTHONY. Oh yeah.
LESLY. You just jiggle it.
ANTHONY. Right. It hasn't worked right since Jackie flushed the lizard.
LESLY. The lizard?
ANTHONY. Marty's lizard.
LESLY. Marty has a lizard?

16

ANTHONY.   Had, had a lizard.

LESLY.   It got in there by mistake?

ANTHONY.   No. On purpose.

LESLY.   It liked the water.

ANTHONY.   I guess. Jackie put it there.

LESLY.   And then she forgot.

ANTHONY.   No, she remembered.

LESLY.   She flushed him on purpose?

ANTHONY.   I think she was jealous. Marty loved that lizard. It turned different colors. Well, I guess you want to do mascara or something.

LESLY.   Yeah.

ANTHONY.   There's bobby pins on the bureau. 'Cause of Emily Post and all.

LESLY.   She stayed here?

ANTHONY.   No. She said a hostess should do her hair in every guest bedroom to see if there was enough light, so my mom did that. And there was. So if you want to do your hair, you're set.

LESLY.   I do.

ANTHONY.   What?

LESLY.   Want to do my hair. 'Cause of the rain and all.

ANTHONY.   It looks nice the way it is.

LESLY.   Come on.

ANTHONY.   Really.

LESLY.   Well I guess I'll see you at dinner.

ANTHONY.   I hope you like turkey 'cause that's what we're having.

LESLY.   Yes. I mean. It's Thanksgiving.

ANTHONY.   Did I show you the toilet thing?

LESLY.   Yeah.

ANTHONY.   And the towels.

LESLY.   They're here.

ANTHONY.   Could you just check and see if there's sheets 'cause my mother was all distracted.

LESLY.   *(Checking.)* Yeah there are.

ANTHONY.   And pillows?

LESLY.   Anthony. I don't mean to be unpolite but I'm kind

of tired? And all? So?

ANTHONY.   Oh I'm sorry. It's just ... we never had a guest before.

LESLY.   Never?

ANTHONY.   Never.

BLACKOUT

Scene 3

The guest bedroom. Lesly is hurriedly getting dressed for dinner.

Marty stands where we last saw Anthony.

LESLY.   *(Urgently, sotto voce.)* The toilet's running.

MARTY.   *(Miming jiggling.)* Did you ...

LESLY.   *Yes* but ...

MARTY.   It'll stop eventually.

LESLY.   It's making a *noise.*

MARTY.   I can't hear it.

LESLY.   It *was.*

MARTY.   What are you doing?

LESLY.   I don't like these shoes.

MARTY.   They look fine.

LESLY.   They skid. I nearly skidded.

MARTY.   Come here.

LESLY.   No.

MARTY.   Why not?

LESLY.   Lipstick.

MARTY.   Reapply. *(Marty kisses her passionately.)* We don't have to stay here.

LESLY.   *Marty.*

MARTY.   What?

LESLY.   It's Thanksgiving.

MARTY.   Nobody cares.

LESLY. But we drove …

MARTY. We can drive back. We could watch the parade.

LESLY. It's rained out.

MARTY. Says who?

LESLY. The news. They showed Bullwinkle. Blowing. He nearly came undone.

MARTY. Now that would be something to see.

LESLY. Where you think he'd end up?

MARTY. I don't know. Outer space?

LESLY. Somebody's backyard probably. *(Marty nuzzles her. Laughing.)* Let go.

MARTY. I love your shoes.

LESLY. Stop.

MARTY. You've met them. They've met you. Let's go.

LESLY. They gave me towels and bobby pins and everything.

MARTY. Bobby pins?

LESLY. It would be rude.

MARTY. They won't care.

LESLY. *(Suddenly worried.)* They don't like me.

MARTY. They love you!

LESLY. I wore the wrong clothes.

MARTY. *No.*

LESLY. I was in a hurricane you know, a person can't look all … when it's raining and blowing and …

MARTY. You looked beautiful, you *are* beautiful, kiss me.

LESLY. They're your *family.*

MARTY. You're my family.

LESLY. Not yet.

BLACKOUT

Scene 4

The guest bedroom. Jackie-O stands where we last saw Marty.

JACKIE-O. Did Marty tell you about me?

LESLY. Oh yes.

JACKIE-O. What did he tell you?

LESLY. He told me how you were.

JACKIE-O. How's that?

LESLY. You know. Glamorous.

JACKIE-O. I spend most of my days with my head in the toilet bowl.

LESLY. Well.

JACKIE-O. Throwing up pills. I can't think when I take the pills and a person needs to think. I mean if a person can't think, what are they?

LESLY. Why are you taking pills?

JACKIE-O. The doctors make me.

LESLY. Have you talked to them? About not being able to think and all.

JACKIE-O. Oh they'd just think I was crazy, not taking my pills. Most doctors are men you know, and they think we're all perpetually premenstrual.

LESLY. Well we are, except when we're actually having it. You know, the visitor.

JACKIE-O. The visitor?

LESLY. That's what I call it.

JACKIE-O. Are you saving yourself for marriage?

LESLY. How do you mean?

JACKIE-O. Blood on the sheets, all that.

LESLY. Well, we live together, Marty and me.

JACKIE-O. That must be hard, saving yourself for marriage when you live together.

LESLY. I'm not. Saving myself.

JACKIE-O. No?

LESLY. Do you think I should of?

JACKIE-O. If I were getting married I'd want to check out the goods.

LESLY. Me too.

JACKIE-O. How were they? The goods.

LESLY. Marty? I can't describe it.

JACKIE-O. I could.

LESLY. What?

JACKIE-O. What's the wildest place you've ever made love?

20

LESLY.   With Marty?

JACKIE-O.   Yes.

LESLY.   I can't talk like that about your *brother*.

JACKIE-O.   Pretend he's not my brother. I do.

LESLY.   Well one time ...

JACKIE-O.   What?

LESLY.   I *can't?*

JACKIE-O.   Why not?

LESLY.   It's embarrassing!

JACKIE-O.   If you don't tell me, I'll just get it out of Marty.

LESLY.   He would never.

JACKIE-O.   What?

LESLY.   Talk like that.

JACKIE-O.   Marty and I tell each other everything.

LESLY.   Everything?

JACKIE-O.   Yes.

LESLY.   Did he tell you about his other girlfriends?

JACKIE-O.   Did he tell *you* about his other girlfriends?

LESLY.   There was one he said.

JACKIE-O.   Did he tell you about her?

LESLY.   No. What was she like? The girl?

JACKIE-O.   She wasn't a girl. She was a woman.

LESLY.   She was older than Marty?

JACKIE-O.   No, they were almost exactly the same age. Talk about glamorous. *She* was glamorous.

LESLY.   I thought so. Is she still here? In Washington?

JACKIE-O.   Very much so. I wonder....

LESLY.   What?

JACKIE-O.   No, it's none of my business.

LESLY.   What?

JACKIE-O.   If he plans to see her while he's home.

LESLY.   Why didn't he marry her?

JACKIE-O.   He couldn't.

LESLY.   Why not?

JACKIE-O.   It was a family thing.

LESLY.   The families objected?

JACKIE-O.   Something like that.

LESLY.   He never told me.

JACKIE-O.   Men and their secrets.

LESLY.   Not all men have secrets.

JACKIE-O.   We all have our secrets.

CROSSFADE

Scene 5

To the living room, where Anthony sits alone. Marty enters.

MARTY.   Where's Jackie-O?

ANTHONY.   In her room.

MARTY.   What's she doing there?

ANTHONY.   I don't know. Brushing her hair?

MARTY.   How is she doing?

ANTHONY.   I don't know. She's in her room.

MARTY.   I mean generally.

ANTHONY.   In general?

MARTY.   Yes.

ANTHONY.   Good. I mean. Good for Jackie.

MARTY.   What does she do all day?

ANTHONY.   I don't know. I mean, what does anybody do all day? What do you do all day? What do I do all day?

MARTY.   What *do* you do all day?

ANTHONY.   I don't know. I guess that's why people keep diaries. So they know. She reads books.

MARTY.   What kind of books?

ANTHONY.   Assassination books.

MARTY.   How many assassination books can there be?

ANTHONY.   A lot. Lincoln, McKinley, Kennedy, King, Kennedy ...

MARTY.   All right.

ANTHONY.   And she watches soap operas. She likes it especially when they have a character and that actress leaves the show and a new actress steps in and becomes the character.

And nobody on the show notices any difference, they treat that character exactly the same as before.

MARTY. Jackie watches soap operas?

ANTHONY. I guess you heard about the seltzer water thing. That was the last big, you know.

MARTY. It was flat?

ANTHONY. Yeah, like when somebody doesn't screw the top back on.

MARTY. So what'd she do?

ANTHONY. Well she started screaming about bubbles, how there were no bubbles, so she started boiling the seltzer water and when the water started bubbling she poured the boiling water back into the seltzer bottle, which was plastic and started to melt and kind of melted into her hand where she was holding it and she had to go to the emergency room with third degree burns. And on the way home, whenever Mama and I asked her a question she'd tell us to stop giving her the third degree and she'd laugh kind of like hysterically. So she's not what you'd call recovered.

MARTY. Do you think I should stay?

JACKIE-O. *(Entering.)* Yes. Yes I do. *(Jackie-O picks up a glass of wine.)*

ANTHONY. You're not supposed to uh, have that.

JACKIE-O. What?

ANTHONY. The wine.

JACKIE-O. Isn't there enough?

ANTHONY. There's enough, but ... *(To Marty.)* She's not supposed to have that.

MARTY. Why not?

ANTHONY. Because of her medication.

JACKIE-O. Not *this* medication, Anthony. The one *before* I couldn't drink. They've switched me. I used to be orange, now I'm blue. I wanted pills to match my eyes. *(Toasting.)* Color me beautiful.

MARTY. Mama wants us to leave. She's afraid I'll push you over the edge.

JACKIE-O. I've been over the edge. Now I'm back.

MARTY. Lesly doesn't know about the hospital.

JACKIE-O. Oh?

MARTY.   She knows about the hospital, but not what kind of hospital.

JACKIE-O.   Does she know about *your* hospital?

MARTY.   Sort of.

JACKIE-O.   Let me guess. You had your appendix out.

ANTHONY.   You did?

MARTY.   No.

JACKIE-O.   Hey Marty, ya wanna show me your scar?

MARTY.   No.

JACKIE-O.   I'm sorry about that by the way. I didn't mean to maim you, I only meant to kill you.

MARTY.   These things happen.

JACKIE-O.   I've noticed Anthony wears a lot of layers around me, don't you Anthony? Look at him. He's got a T-shirt, a vest, and a jacket.

ANTHONY.   I'm wearing the jacket 'cause it's Thanksgiving.

JACKIE-O.   You weren't wearing it before.

ANTHONY.   I put it on after Marty got here.

MARTY.   It looks nice.

ANTHONY.   I got it at the Treasure Trove. I think it belonged to a Kennedy.

JACKIE-O.   Why? Is there a bullet hole?

MARTY.   Jackie.

ANTHONY.   The lady said Mrs. Kennedy donated a bunch of stuff. She was pretty sure this was in the Kennedy batch.

JACKIE-O.   You see Marty, you've turned the household upside down. Anthony went out and bought a jacket, I went to a lot of trouble to get sane, so you can't just leave. Lesly, on the other hand, is free to go at any time. *(A window bangs.)*

ANTHONY.   I've never been to a hurricane before, have you?

JACKIE-O and MARTY.   Yes.

ANTHONY.   When?

JACKIE-O.   It was before you were born. We went to Virginia Beach and our motel was right on the water. Mom and Dad were drinking rum and Pepsi out of Styrofoam cups and giggling.

ANTHONY.   All the good things happened before I got born.

JACKIE-O.   This wine is not very cold.

ANTHONY.   Mom forgot to put it in the icebox.

JACKIE-O.   I wish I had a piece of ice.

ANTHONY.   I'll get you one.

JACKIE-O.   Don't you go Anthony. Marty, fetch me a piece of ice, will you?

ANTHONY.   I'll get it for you.

JACKIE-O.   Marty's been in the car all day, I'm sure he'd leap at an opportunity to stretch his legs.

ANTHONY.   He doesn't know where we keep the ice.

JACKIE-O.   Everyone knows where you keep the ice, Anthony.

MARTY.   *(Softly, to Jackie-O.)* Are you gonna be good when Lesly comes down?

JACKIE-O.   Marty, I'm the hostess. *(Marty exits.)*

ANTHONY.   *(Calling after him.)* And make sure it's cold!

JACKIE-O.   She's pretty, isn't she?

ANTHONY.   Who?

JACKIE-O.   Who do you think?

ANTHONY.   I guess.

JACKIE-O.   She doesn't seem like Marty's type. Do you think she seems like Marty's type?

ANTHONY.   I don't know.

JACKIE-O.   Now you and she would make a cute couple. Why, I'll bet you're just the same age.

ANTHONY.   They're getting married Jackie. She's got a ring.

JACKIE-O.   Tiffany's?

ANTHONY.   I don't know!

JACKIE-O.   I think she has a sneak for you.

ANTHONY.   Stop.

JACKIE-O.   I do.

ANTHONY.   She's *engaged. (Marty enters, carrying an ice cube.)*

JACKIE-O.   Oh Anthony look, isn't that the prettiest ice cube you've ever seen?

MARTY.   It used to be bigger.

JACKIE-O.   I wonder what happened.

MARTY.   Whatever it was it happened just between the kitchen and here.

JACKIE-O.   Look Marty, your hands are all wet. Now that's a clue.

LESLY.   *(Entering.)* It probably melted. On the way. *(Pause. They all turn to look at her.)*

JACKIE-O.   Oh my. Good evening.

LESLY.   Good evening.

JACKIE-O.   Is that an evening dress?

LESLY.   I don't know.

JACKIE-O.   It certainly looks like an evening dress.

ANTHONY.   It's very pretty.

LESLY.   I dressed for dinner.

ANTHONY.   Would you like a glass of Liebfraumilch?

LESLY.   No thank you, I'll just have a glass of wine.

MARTY.   *(Quietly.)* That's the name of the wine.

LESLY.   Oh. *(Laughing nervously.)* I don't speak French.

JACKIE-O.   Who does?

ANTHONY.   You do.

JACKIE-O.   Oh that's right, I do.

LESLY.   What does the name mean?

JACKIE-O.   In French I think it means something German.

LESLY.   Oh.

MARTY.   It means "loving mother's milk."

LESLY.   You speak French?

MARTY.   No. German. *(Pause.)*

LESLY.   I know how to say "I love you" in sign language.

ANTHONY.   Let's see. *(Lesly signs "I love you.")* Cool.

JACKIE-O.   Don't leave this girl alone with any handsome deaf-mutes Marty, that's my advice to you.

MARTY.   Jackie.

JACKIE-O.   Tell me Lesly, have you ever been to Washington before?

LESLY.   No.

JACKIE-O.   Not even on a field trip? Not even on your fifth grade field trip?

LESLY.   No. I mean my class went but I didn't go.

JACKIE-O.   In fifth grade? Really?

MARTY.   Sixth. Sixth grade.

JACKIE-O.   So you just snubbed it. You just snubbed your

nation's capitol.

LESLY.   My parents wouldn't let me go.

JACKIE-O.   What's their number?

LESLY.   What?

JACKIE-O.   How could they have ruined a perfectly good field trip? Really. People like that burn me up. Don't they burn you up Marty?

MARTY.   They didn't have the money.

JACKIE-O.   What a lie. How much could it have cost?

MARTY.   Too much.

LESLY.   My father was unemployed. My father was laid off.

JACKIE-O.   Were you poor? Did you eat chicken pot pies?

LESLY.   Pancakes. A lot of pancakes.

JACKIE-O.   Pancakes. Pancakes, Marty. And how did you pull yourself out? Out of poverty I mean.

LESLY.   I left Pennsylvania.

JACKIE-O.   That was a step in the right direction. Clearly. *(Lesly looks at the paintings hung on the wall.)* Do they have paintings in Pennsylvania?

MARTY.   Jackie.

JACKIE-O.   Well Marty I've never been to Pennsylvania, I've never even *met* anybody who's been to Pennsylvania, much less been *from* Pennsylvania, Pennsylvania is just this state that gets in your way when you have to go someplace else!

LESLY.   Why do they call you Jackie-O?

JACKIE-O.   We went to an Ides of March party. I went as Jackie Onassis. In a pink Chanel suit and a pillbox hat. And blood … on my dress.

LESLY.   Blood?

JACKIE-O.   And other stuff too. Like macaroni. Kind of glued on. Like brains. *(Pause.)*

LESLY.   I don't think that's funny.

JACKIE-O.   Nobody else did either. Nobody talked to me all night.

MARTY.   I talked to you.

JACKIE-O.   Yes. You talked to me. Marty. Jackie-O wants a drink drink. Let's drink rum and Pepsi out of Styrofoam cups. Anthony, come on darling, let's drink rum and Pepsi out of

Styrofoam cups. Bring in some ice!

MARTY.   We're out of ice.

JACKIE-O.   How can we be out of ice?

MARTY.   Mama forgot to fill the ice trays. I gave you the last cube.

JACKIE-O.   I thought this was the modern world. I thought that in the modern world a person could get whatever they wanted.

ANTHONY.   The Pepsi's cold.

JACKIE-O.   It's not the same. I'm not talking about ice, I'm talking about texture! I'm talking about texture! In the last hurricane we had ice. Mama and Daddy had a bucket of ice and a cooler down the hall. We just marched down the hall whenever we had a yen for ice. *(There is a trace of hysteria in Jackie-O's voice. Marty crosses to her and soothes her like a child. Anthony hovers nervously. Lesly watches.)*

MARTY.   Jackie. Jackie-O. Marty's here.

JACKIE-O.   A person gets her heart set on a certain thing ...

MARTY.   Yes ...

JACKIE-O.   A person gets her heart set on a certain thing ...

MARTY.   Yes ...

JACKIE-O.   And if a certain person can't get the thing her heart is set on, a certain person goes insane. *(To Lesly, suddenly matter-of-fact.)* I suppose you think I'm going insane just to be fashionable.

LESLY.   I don't think you're insane.

JACKIE-O.   You don't think I'm insane?

LESLY.   No.

JACKIE-O.   You don't think I'm just an eensy-weensy bit insane?

LESLY.   I don't think you're insane. I think you're spoiled.

JACKIE-O.   Oh please. If people are gonna start telling the truth I'm going to bed. *(The lights flicker then go out. Pause.)*

LESLY.   Does this happen alot?

JACKIE-O.   Every hurricane.

ANTHONY.   We bought emergency candles. They're right in this drawer. *(Enter Mrs. Pascal.)*

MRS. PASCAL.   Anthony, did we remember to buy matches?

ANTHONY.   Nobody *buys* matches, people *find* matches.

MRS. PASCAL.   People buy matches, Anthony, but not people like us. People like us forget to buy matches.

LESLY.   You could light them on the stove.

MRS. PASCAL.   Electric. Electric stove. Oh my God.

ANTHONY.   What?

MRS. PASCAL.   Dinner. Thanksgiving dinner.

ANTHONY.   There's matches in the bathroom. *(Marty exits into the bathroom.)*

MRS. PASCAL.   Why are there matches in the bathroom?

ANTHONY.   For the smell. When somebody does one.

JACKIE-O.   That's not why they're in the bathroom.

ANTHONY.   It's not?

JACKIE-O.   It's for my scent candle.

ANTHONY.   It is?

JACKIE-O.   "When somebody does one." God.

MARTY.   *(Re-entering.)* I got them. Where's the candles? *(Anthony hands Marty a candle. He lights it.)*

MRS. PASCAL.   If I had put the turkey in one hour earlier we'd be impervious.

LESLY.   We ate at McDonald's anyway.

MRS. PASCAL.   What?

LESLY.   On the way. At a rest stop.

MRS. PASCAL.   Well.

LESLY.   We got hungry.

MRS. PASCAL.   Does anybody want any cranberry sauce?

ANTHONY.   Just cranberry sauce?

MRS. PASCAL.   You can eat it raw.

LESLY.   It's not really raw. It's been pre-cooked.

MRS. PASCAL.   Jackie, is that a drink you're drinking?

JACKIE-O.   This drink?

MRS. PASCAL.   Yes.

JACKIE-O.   No.

MRS. PASCAL.   Anthony, is that a drink she's drinking?

ANTHONY.   It's Liebfraumilch.

MRS. PASCAL.   Take it away from her.

ANTHONY.   She said she switched medication.

MRS. PASCAL.   She's mistaken. Take it away. Jackie, you look tired, why don't you go to bed?

JACKIE-O.   I get bored in bed.

MRS. PASCAL.   Well *I'm* going to bed and I think everyone should do the same.

ANTHONY.   It's still early.

MRS. PASCAL.   There's no television and no food. What is there to stay up for?

ANTHONY.   Conversation.

MRS. PASCAL.   Oh *that*, that only gets you into trouble. Take it from one who knows. Give me a candle and I shall find my way. Never mind, I'll just curse the darkness. *(Mrs. Pascal exits.)*

LESLY.   It's been a long day.

JACKIE-O.   Not as long as yesterday. Yesterday was 24 hours.

LESLY.   I meant with the traveling and all.

JACKIE-O.   It's no easier staying in one place. Take it from one who knows.

MARTY.   Was that wise? I think that was wise.

JACKIE-O.   I knew it would happen. One day I'd just wake up wise.

MARTY.   One day I woke up stupid.

JACKIE-O.   You did?

MARTY.   It was terrible.

JACKIE-O.   What did you do?

MARTY.   I went back to sleep.

JACKIE-O.   That was wise.

LESLY.   I'm tired Marty. I'm going up now. Are you coming up?

MARTY.   Soon. *(Lesly hesitates for a moment and then exits. Anthony calls after her.)*

ANTHONY.   Clean towels and a washcloth are laid out on the bed! Yell down if you need anything! *(Marty and Jackie-O smile.)* What?

MARTY.   *(To Jackie-O.)* I got your letter.

JACKIE-O.   Oh?

MARTY.   I've forgotten his name. The one who was lousy in bed.

ANTHONY.   Who was lousy in bed?

30

MARTY.   But to be lousy in bed, you have to be in bed, don't you?

ANTHONY.   Who was lousy in bed?

JACKIE-O.   That actor.

ANTHONY. Peter? Peter was lousy in bed? I can't believe it.

MARTY.   Tell me about Peter, Anthony.

ANTHONY.   He wears black. And he has a gap between his teeth. His eyes are green and one eye is squinty. Like sexy, not like disfigured. He's in love with Jackie, you can tell. If he gets to hold her coat for her, his heart breaks into a million pieces on the floor.

MARTY.   So Peter's in love with Jackie-O.

JACKIE-O.   Don't use that word.

MARTY.   What word?

JACKIE-O.   Love. Love is for tiny people with tiny lives. Peter and I have nothing in common. Now you and I Marty, have a great deal in common. Parents, DNA, bone structure.

ANTHONY.   He doesn't look like he'd be lousy in bed.

JACKIE-O.   Now Anthony, we have something to tell you ...

MARTY.   Let's talk about Anthony. Let's express some familial concern about Anthony. Now Anthony, why aren't you at school?

ANTHONY.   I dropped out.

MARTY.   *(To Jackie-O.)* He dropped out.

JACKIE-O.   Yes I know.

MARTY.   Why did you drop out Anthony?

ANTHONY.   Why didn't you go with her Marty?

MARTY.   Excuse me Anthony, but we're talking about you now. We're expressing Familial Concern.

ANTHONY.   No you're not.

MARTY.   We're not?

ANTHONY.   You're playing the Familial Concern game.

JACKIE-O.   Oh Anthony, don't be sincere, it's déclassé.

ANTHONY.   I hear you crying at night alone in your room. *(To Marty.)* I hear her crying at night alone in her room.

MARTY.   *(To Jackie-O.)* You cry at night alone in your room?

ANTHONY.   Don't make fun of her! I won't let you make fun of her!

31

MARTY.   I wasn't going to make fun of her. I was going to ask her what she cries about.

JACKIE-O.   You want somebody for a very long time and then you have them and they love you and they make love to you but it's not enough. This is the truth about sex.

ANTHONY.   Is that why Peter was lousy in bed?

JACKIE-O.   I'm not talking about Peter, Anthony. I'm talking about Marty. I'm talking about Marty. *(Pause.)*

ANTHONY.   Why did you tell me! I wish you hadn't told me.

JACKIE-O.   Anthony, you knew ...

ANTHONY.   I did not know! How old were you?

JACKIE-O.   Young.

ANTHONY.   My whole life?

JACKIE-O.   Practically your whole life.

ANTHONY.   I felt left out.

JACKIE-O.   Little brothers always feel left out.

ANTHONY.   I felt majorly left out! Is that why you went crazy?

JACKIE-O.   No.

ANTHONY.   That's why you went crazy. You were ashamed.

JACKIE-O.   I wasn't ashamed.

ANTHONY.   Well you should be!

JACKIE-O.   Don't be bourgeois, Anthony.

ANTHONY.   I'm not being bourgeois! Don't call me bourgeois just 'cause I know right from wrong! *(To Marty.)* Does Lesly know?

MARTY.   No.

ANTHONY.   Well are you gonna tell her?

MARTY.   No.

ANTHONY.   You're *not* gonna tell her?

MARTY.   How can I tell her?

ANTHONY.   You just ... tell her.

MARTY.   Why?

ANTHONY.   So she knows.

JACKIE-O.   I'll tell her.

MARTY.   Don't.

JACKIE-O.   She'll understand. She's from Pennsylvania. Entire towns are related.

ANTHONY. That's like cousins.

JACKIE-O. So?

ANTHONY. So you're not cousins. You're twins.

JACKIE-O. That explains a great deal. Why Mama insists on celebrating our birthdays on the same day for example. I thought she was just being chintzy with the party favors.

ANTHONY. It would be bad enough if you were brother and sister but *twins* ...

JACKIE-O. Your moral outrage is very specific, Anthony ...

ANTHONY. It's like fucking a mirror! *(Pause.)*

JACKIE-O. Anthony said "fuck."

MARTY. I know. I heard.

JACKIE-O. Fucking a mirror. That sounds painful.

ANTHONY. *(To Marty.)* Go upstairs. Go upstairs and tell her or I'll ...

MARTY. What?

ANTHONY. Be really mad. *(Pause. Anthony exits. Jackie-O goes to kiss Marty.)*

MARTY. Don't.

JACKIE-O. What?

MARTY. Do that.

JACKIE-O. Okay, let's do something else. Let's do mime.

MARTY. No. *(Jackie-O does a conventional box mime.)*

JACKIE-O. Guess where I am? I'm in a box and I can't get out.

MARTY. No, *I'm* in a box and I can't get out.

JACKIE-O. Well I'm sorry, that wasn't a very good mime, Marty, because I didn't see that at all.

MARTY. Why did you have to tell him?

JACKIE-O. To get him out of the room.

MARTY. What if he tells Lesly?

JACKIE-O. He won't.

MARTY. What if he does?

JACKIE-O. Are you ashamed?

MARTY. Of what?

JACKIE-O. Of us. Of what we have.

MARTY. Had.

JACKIE-O. I don't recognize the past tense.

MARTY.   I'm not ashamed.

JACKIE-O.   What are you?

MARTY.   I don't know. I see other houses, I see other lives and ...

JACKIE-O.   What?

MARTY.   They're not like mine.

JACKIE-O.   They're not like mine either.

MARTY.   They could be.

JACKIE-O.   Other lives don't interest me.

MARTY.   That's what we always said, but maybe we said that because we thought we couldn't have it, maybe ...

JACKIE-O.   We could all move to Pennsylvania.

MARTY.   I should go up soon.

JACKIE-O.   We're not going to bed until one of three things happens. The hurricane ends or we run out of rum.

MARTY.   That's two. *(Jackie-O smiles slowly at him.)*

CROSSFADE

Scene 6

The guest bedroom. Lesly is unpacking. Anthony stands in the doorway.

ANTHONY.   I have to talk to you.

LESLY.   About what?

ANTHONY.   Stuff.

LESLY.   Okay, but I'm unpacking.

ANTHONY.   Can I help?

LESLY.   No, that's okay.

ANTHONY.   Why not?

LESLY.   There's, you know, girl stuff.

ANTHONY.   Tampons?

LESLY.   Anthony.

ANTHONY.   Underwear?

LESLY.   What did you want to talk to me about?

ANTHONY. Where did you meet Marty?

LESLY. At a party.

ANTHONY. What kind of party?

LESLY. Like, a party someone has in their house, you know. Apartment.

ANTHONY. What did he say and what did you say?

LESLY. Well there were no chairs. There were two chairs. Boat chairs, like those chairs they have on boats. So Marty was sitting in one. And then he got up. You know. To give me the chair. I knew he wasn't from New York.

ANTHONY. So you fell in love with him.

LESLY. No. I thought he was gay.

ANTHONY. You did? Why?

LESLY. Well everyone is. In New York. I mean not me. But everyone. Men. And he was so beautiful, you know.

ANTHONY. Do you think I am? Beautiful.

LESLY. Well you look like Marty.

ANTHONY. I do?

LESLY. Uh-huh.

ANTHONY. 'Cause we're not exactly sure we had the same father. I mean my mother always had the same husband. But she was kind of a free spirit. You know. Like that.

LESLY. Doesn't that bother you?

ANTHONY. Well I mean if it did it wouldn't change anything. I mean I don't mean to be Buddhistic or anything.

LESLY. Be what?

ANTHONY. Buddhistic.

LESLY. Oh, that's okay.

ANTHONY. How old are you?

LESLY. Twenty-three.

ANTHONY. Me too.

LESLY. Oh. I thought you were younger.

ANTHONY. Well. I am. What do you think about sex?

LESLY. Well I mean, sex is good with the right man. But you have to be careful, you know. Especially in New York.

ANTHONY. Careful?

LESLY. Diseases. Like that.

ANTHONY. Mental diseases?

LESLY. No.

ANTHONY. But you should be careful of mental diseases too.

LESLY. I guess.

ANTHONY. If somebody else fell in love with you now, what would you do?

LESLY. Tell them I was engaged.

ANTHONY. You wouldn't, you wouldn't maybe check it out, see if maybe he's got something to offer or ... like that.

LESLY. No.

ANTHONY. Do I have a fever? *(Lesly puts her hand on his forehead and sits beside him.)*

LESLY. No.

ANTHONY. Are you sure?

LESLY. I'm pretty sure.

ANTHONY. Can you check again? *(Lesly checks again.)*

LESLY. Well you're warm, but not like a fever. More like ... warm.

ANTHONY. It's because I'm sitting next to you. I'm warm because I'm sitting next to you.

LESLY. Anthony.

ANTHONY. What?

LESLY. You know. Like I said.

ANTHONY. Lesly. Can I hold your hand? Just hold your hand?

LESLY. Okay.

ANTHONY. What's that?

LESLY. A scar.

ANTHONY. From what?

LESLY. A cheese knife. I was cutting cheese.

ANTHONY. That's it? That's the story?

LESLY. Uh huh.

ANTHONY. I have a scar. Here. *(He points to his neck.)* Marty and Jackie were playing French Revolution and they made me play Marie Antoinette. I probably have mental scars too. Mental scar tissue.

LESLY. Marty's probably gonna be coming up pretty soon.

ANTHONY. I don't think so. He's with Jackie-O.

LESLY. So?

36

ANTHONY. Can I hold something else now?

LESLY. *Anthony.*

ANTHONY. Can I see your knees?

LESLY. No.

ANTHONY. I like that expression "bee's knees." Like "I think you're the bee's knees."

LESLY. Bees don't have knees.

ANTHONY. Tell me about when you lost your virginity.

LESLY. No.

ANTHONY. Tell me something.

LESLY. I don't know what to tell you.

ANTHONY. Anything. *(Pause.)*

LESLY. In fourth grade, Cindy McKinney, she was this girl, she always wore a purple bra with a white shirt, you know?

ANTHONY. No. What?

LESLY. Like she was showing off that she had a bra, you know.

ANTHONY. Oh.

LESLY. I hate people like that.

ANTHONY. Me too. Cindy McKinney, huh?

LESLY. Yeah.

ANTHONY. Whatever happened to old Cindy McKinney?

LESLY. I don't know.

ANTHONY. *Purple.* I hate that.

LESLY. Me too.

ANTHONY. Do I have a fever?

LESLY. I already checked. Before. Twice.

ANTHONY. I know but this time I think I really have one.

LESLY. *(Checking his forehead.)* You're warm. But not like burning up.

ANTHONY. I think I have a brain tumor.

LESLY. You do?

ANTHONY. And you know what the big tragedy of that is?

LESLY. You'll die?

ANTHONY. Yeah. But I'll die without ever having ... you know.

LESLY. You've never...?

ANTHONY. No.

37

LESLY. I thought you went to Princeton.

ANTHONY. Only for two months.

LESLY. It's not that big a tragedy. I mean unless you're with exactly the right person it's not that great.

ANTHONY. It's not that great?

LESLY. No. Like if they smoke they taste like ashes. Like that. Or they like stick their tongue in your ear so much you get like chapped ears.

ANTHONY. Wow.

LESLY. Or like they start and you have to go to the bathroom.

ANTHONY. Lesly.

LESLY. Huh?

ANTHONY. I don't smoke. I won't stick my tongue in your ear and if you have to go we'll just stop and then when you come back we'll start again.

LESLY. Anthony, it's too weird. Doing it with two brothers is like incest.

ANTHONY. Lesly. About incest. I have two words to say to you. Jackie-O and Marty. Jackie-O and Marty. *(Lesly's head slowly turns towards him.)*

LESLY. How do you know that?

ANTHONY. They *told* me.

LESLY. Who told you?

ANTHONY. Jackie.

LESLY. Ha.

ANTHONY. Then Marty. Marty too. *(Lesly is silent.)* Are you okay?

LESLY. *(Softly.)* No.

ANTHONY. Sweetie?

LESLY. Why'd you call me that?

ANTHONY. I don't know. It just came out.

LESLY. My Dad used to call me that. Before.

ANTHONY. Before what?

LESLY. Before he died.

ANTHONY. I could call you that again.

LESLY. That's okay. I don't know what to do.

ANTHONY. I could stay with you.

LESLY.   Stay with me how?

ANTHONY.   Anyway you want me to stay with you.

LESLY.   With your clothes on?

ANTHONY.   Or off. *(Pause. Lesly looks at him.)*

LESLY.   You look like Marty.

ANTHONY.   You look like Lesly. Lesly? I love you, Lesly. *(Anthony begins to kiss her hair and her cheeks. She allows him to. She sighs and offers her lips to be kissed. Mrs. Pascal appears unseen and watches, a cocktail glass in her hand. We hear the amplified sound of ice tinkling.)*

BLACKOUT

Scene 7

The guest bedroom. Anthony is sleeping, wearing only boxer shorts. Lesly sits on the side of the bed, dressing.

ANTHONY.   *(Sleepily.)* Where are you going?

LESLY.   To find Marty.

ANTHONY.   He's not in his room.

LESLY.   How do you know?

ANTHONY.   When I went to the bathroom his door was open. *(Pause.)* Lesly, was I terrible?

LESLY.   *(Kissing him on the head.)* You were fine.

ANTHONY.   Fine?

LESLY.   Just fine.

ANTHONY.   You mean "just fine" or "just" fine?

LESLY.   It was your first time.

ANTHONY.   It's supposed to last longer, isn't it?

LESLY.   Eventually.

ANTHONY.   How long does like Marty last?

LESLY.   *Anthony.*

ANTHONY.   What?

LESLY.   That's personal.

ANTHONY.   You won't tell him, will you?

LESLY. What?

ANTHONY. How I was.

LESLY. No.

ANTHONY. But you're gonna tell him? About us?

LESLY. I don't know.

ANTHONY. What about honesty, the importance of honesty in a relationship? I'll always be honest with you, Lesly.

LESLY. Oh.

ANTHONY. Always.

LESLY. Well. Thank you.

ANTHONY. You looked different with your clothes off.

LESLY. You're supposed to.

ANTHONY. I mean different from the way I imagined your body with your clothes off with your clothes on. You have muscles. You could work like on a farm.

LESLY. I did.

ANTHONY. Like those Soviet women with the kerchiefs.

LESLY. The fat ones?

ANTHONY. No, the ones with the kerchiefs.

LESLY. Russian women are fat. *(Lesly stands.)*

ANTHONY. Your shirt is on inside out.

LESLY. I always do that.

ANTHONY. Turn on the light if you want.

LESLY. The electricity's out.

ANTHONY. Maybe it's back. Try the light.

LESLY. I don't want to.

ANTHONY. Why not?

LESLY. I'm shy.

ANTHONY. Lesly, we just …

LESLY. That's different. That was just something I did. You have to be with someone for a while before you let them really look at you.

ANTHONY. Do you let Marty look at you?

LESLY. Of course. Damn. I broke my heel.

ANTHONY. Here. Give it to me. I have Crazy Glue.

LESLY. How long does that take?

ANTHONY. I have to read the instructions. It works overnight.

LESLY. That's too long. I'll just go barefoot.

ANTHONY. Wait. Let me fix it for you. It doesn't need overnight. That was a lie. *(She hands him the shoe.)*

LESLY. Anthony, not five minutes ago, you said you would always be honest with me.

ANTHONY. I lied. To keep you here.

LESLY. I can't stay here. And you can't stay here. I was confused before. I was in a state of confusion.

ANTHONY. That's 'cause we were in the heat of passion.

LESLY. I wasn't in the heat of passion.

ANTHONY. I'm closing my ears.

LESLY. I was pretending you were Marty. But it didn't work. You're brothers but you smell different, taste different, everything.

ANTHONY. How do I smell?

LESLY. Clean. Like a laundromat.

ANTHONY. And Marty?

LESLY. Champagne.

ANTHONY. What else?

LESLY. I missed the scar.

ANTHONY. Jackie's scar?

LESLY. No, Marty's. On his stomach. From when he had his appendix out.

ANTHONY. Marty had his appendix out?

LESLY. Didn't he?

ANTHONY. No. Jackie shot him.

LESLY. Stop.

ANTHONY. She did.

LESLY. Why?

ANTHONY. 'Cause she felt like it. He was gonna go to New York and she didn't want him to go.

LESLY. Is my shoe ready?

ANTHONY. I just glued it.

LESLY. Give it to me.

ANTHONY. No. It won't hold. You'll fall down the stairs.

LESLY. I'll be careful.

ANTHONY. If you go down there, you may see something.

LESLY. I know.

ANTHONY. Carnal.

LESLY. I *know.*

ANTHONY. So why put yourself through it? Wait till the morning and then tell him it's over.

LESLY. What's over?

ANTHONY. It.

LESLY. Us?

ANTHONY. No. Him. You and him.

LESLY. It's not over Anthony, *we're* over.

ANTHONY. I know.

LESLY. No. *We're* over. You and me.

ANTHONY. Over? How can we be over?

LESLY. We just are. Can I have my shoe?

ANTHONY. No.

LESLY. Fine. *(Lesly limps out. She closes the door behind her. Anthony hurls the shoe at the door.)*

CROSSFADE

Scene 8

The living room.

JACKIE-O. There is something I've been meaning to ask you. There's this thing I've heard and if I thought for one second it were true I would probably kill myself. Does your fiancee work in a donut shop?

MARTY. A Donut King. Actually.

JACKIE-O. A Donut King. So is she like the Queen? Are we entertaining royalty?

MARTY. She would be like a donut lady-in-waiting.

JACKIE-O. So she's sort of a marginal donut figure?

MARTY. In all fairness she is a minor and not a major donut figure. Because it's a chain you see, and there are women just like her all over the city.

JACKIE-O. My point exactly.

MARTY.   No *my* point, my point Jackie. There are women just like her all over the city. I know that. But this one belongs to me. I have chosen to love her, it wasn't thrust upon me by ...

JACKIE-O.   Destiny?

MARTY.   I'm going to bed.

JACKIE-O.   Can I come?

MARTY.   No. *(Jackie-O moves to kiss him.)* Jackie. I love her.

JACKIE-O.   *(Disdainfully.)* Love.

MARTY.   Yes, love, love! I am tired of being above everything! I want to be a human being!

JACKIE-O.   Okay. Let's be human beings.

MARTY.   You don't know how. *(Jackie-O begins to cry.)*

JACKIE-O.   *(Softly.)* You didn't come. To my hospital. You didn't come.

MARTY.   I came.

JACKIE-O.   They didn't tell me.

MARTY.   I came at night. I stood under your window. I watched you put on your make-up. I watched you cry it off. And I knew. I was the one making you crazy. So I left. I went to New York.

JACKIE-O.   But I'm not crazy now, I'm better! I watch soap operas, I bake brownies. Normalcy is coursing through my veins!

MARTY.   I want you to have a life. I want you to love someone you're allowed to love.

JACKIE-O.   I miss you. I miss you so much.

MARTY.   I miss you.

JACKIE-O.   When I was with Peter, I couldn't come without seeing your face. When you make love to that Lesly-girl do you see my face?

MARTY.   Sometimes.

JACKIE-O.   My face how? From when?

MARTY.   The night we went to the party, the Ides of March party. You ran into the room in your slip and pillbox hat ...

JACKIE-O.   And heels, I got to wear heels ...

MARTY.   And Mama's stockings with the seams. You sat down on the couch ...

JACKIE-O. I was waiting for my skirt, the macaroni wouldn't dry ...

MARTY. I followed the seams of your stockings and then I was afraid ...

JACKIE-O. So I began the game. Marty. Look. *(Jackie-O puts on a pink pillbox hat.)*

MARTY. You look lovely.

JACKIE-O. I have everything. The dress. Everything.

MARTY. The dress?

JACKIE-O. The suit. I could put it on.

MARTY. Don't.

JACKIE-O. For old time's sake. *(Jackie-O begins to dress in a 1960's pink Chanel suit.)*

MARTY. Lesly may come down.

JACKIE-O. She won't come down.

MARTY. How do you know?

JACKIE-O. She won't come down. I have the gun. *(Jackie-O pulls out a gun.)*

MARTY. Put it down.

JACKIE-O. There's no bullets, Marty. See for yourself. *(Marty checks the gun.)*

MARTY. But the blank, they'll hear the blank.

JACKIE-O. In the storm?

MARTY. It's getting quiet.

JACKIE-O. We're in the eye.

MARTY. Do you still remember that day?

JACKIE-O. The day of the party?

MARTY. The day he was shot.

JACKIE-O. The radio was on, the TV was on.

MARTY. Mama was crying and Daddy was crying.

JACKIE-O. And Daddy was leaving.

MARTY. Finally leaving.

JACKIE-O. She covered him with her body. She tried to keep him there.

MARTY. She tried to keep his head on, but it was falling off.

JACKIE-O. You be him and I'll be her.

MARTY. I'm him?

JACKIE-O.   And I'm her. *(Jackie-O points the gun at him and shoots. He falls. In slow motion they re-enact the moments after Kennedy was assassinated. Jackie-O cradles Marty's head in her lap. Then she straddles him. Marty slowly sits up as Jackie-O arches her back and moves in for a kiss. Lesly stands in the doorway watching.)*

BLACKOUT

Scene 9

The guest bedroom. Lesly enters, out of breath, whimpering. She slams the door and leans against it. She looks up and starts as she realizes Mrs. Pascal is sitting on the bed where she'd left Anthony.

MRS. PASCAL.   You're not bleeding.
LESLY.   No.
MRS. PASCAL.   Who's bleeding?
LESLY.   Nobody.
MRS. PASCAL.   Thank God.
LESLY.   Where's Anthony?
MRS. PASCAL.   Why?
LESLY.   I have to talk to him!
MRS. PASCAL.   *(Standing up.)* There's croissants in the kitchen. They're filled with something. I forget what. You can eat yours in the cab.
LESLY.   I'm not taking a cab.
MRS. PASCAL.   How are you getting to the train?
LESLY.   I'm not taking the train.
MRS. PASCAL.   Then how are you getting back to New York?
LESLY.   Marty will drive me.
MRS. PASCAL.   Marty's needed here.
LESLY.   Marty's needed there!
MRS. PASCAL.   Oh you'll find a replacement.
LESLY.   No I won't.

MRS. PASCAL.   You already have. *(Beat.)*

LESLY.   Were you *spying* on us?

MRS. PASCAL.   A mother doesn't spy. A mother pays attention.

LESLY.   Marty won't let me go without him. He loves me!

MRS. PASCAL.   You're just a symbol to him. A symbol of all that is good and pure.

LESLY.   I'm not a symbol!

MRS. PASCAL.   Not any more.

LESLY.   Please don't tell him about Anthony, it will only hurt him.

MRS. PASCAL.   It's a little late to worry about hurting Marty.

LESLY.   He never has to know.

MRS. PASCAL.   You can see that Jackie-O's a very sick girl. She needs her family.

LESLY.   She has you, she has Anthony.

MRS. PASCAL.   We're beside the point as far as Jackie-O's concerned.

LESLY.   Jackie-O should learn she can't always have everything her way.

MRS. PASCAL.   Jackie *can* have everything her way. She always has.

LESLY.   Is that how you raised them?

MRS. PASCAL.   People "raise" cattle, children just happen.

LESLY.   They don't just *happen.*

MRS. PASCAL.   You can read Dr. Spock from now till Doomsday but children just happen all the same. This one has blue eyes and that one's insane.

LESLY.   Well she can't have Marty. Marty's mine.

MRS. PASCAL.   Oh please, Marty's maybe been sort of yours for six months. He's belonged to Jackie for 20-odd years.

LESLY.   *Very* odd.

MRS. PASCAL.   Leave this morning or Marty finds out where you spent the night. Leave now with your symbology in tact or stay and lose Marty anyway.

LESLY.   So what if I slept with his brother! He slept with his sister!

MRS. PASCAL. I'm sure I don't know what you're talking about.

LESLY. I'm sure you do.

MRS. PASCAL. Sure? One can never be sure. Don't forget your toothbrush.

BLACKOUT

Scene 10

A few moments later. Anthony stands where we last saw Mrs. Pascal. Lesly searches the room wildly.

ANTHONY. What? What? What?

LESLY. The suitcase.

ANTHONY. What suitcase?

LESLY. The blue suitcase, my suitcase, where is it?

ANTHONY. Under the bed. Did you see them?

LESLY. What?

ANTHONY. Jackie, Marty.

LESLY. Uh-huh.

ANTHONY. Was I right, was it carnal?

LESLY. Yes, no, I don't know.

ANTHONY. I told you not to go, didn't I tell you not to go? *(Lesly hurriedly packs her suitcase.)* I'm worried, I'm worried sick. You can't leave like this, in a hurricane.

LESLY. I've got to get Marty out of here.

ANTHONY. Can I come? I want to go to New York. I like the way it smells.

LESLY. Nobody likes the way it smells.

ANTHONY. I do. Like pretzels. Street pretzels.

LESLY. You can't come with us.

ANTHONY. Why?

LESLY. We live in a studio.

ANTHONY. I'm talking about love and you're talking real estate.

LESLY. I don't love you Anthony.

ANTHONY. Fine. Pass the salt. Pour it on my body. Turn me inside out like a slug.

LESLY. What's a slug?

ANTHONY. You don't know what a slug is?

LESLY. Is it like a potato bug?

ANTHONY. What's a potato bug?

LESLY. They live under flagstones.

ANTHONY. Like patios?

LESLY. Yeah.

ANTHONY. Put that back.

LESLY. What?

ANTHONY. That hairbrush.

LESLY. It's my hairbrush.

ANTHONY. It is not.

LESLY. It is too.

ANTHONY. Where'd you buy it?

LESLY. I don't remember …

ANTHONY. Yeah. Right.

LESLY. Macy's! I bought it at Macy's!

ANTHONY. Put everything back. Don't leave. *(Anthony starts to take everything out of her suitcase. She tries to put it back in. He pulls her down on the bed beside him.)* How can you stay with him when you *know, you know?*

LESLY. I don't know I don't know! *(Pause.)*

ANTHONY. We could go to Pennsylvania.

LESLY. What would we do in Pennsylvania?

ANTHONY. We could become Amish people.

LESLY. You can't just become Amish.

ANTHONY. What's the name of your town?

LESLY. You've never heard of it.

ANTHONY. But I want to. Hear of it.

LESLY. It's called Home.

ANTHONY. It is not.

LESLY. It is.

ANTHONY. Really?

LESLY. Really.

ANTHONY. What does that *mean?*

LESLY.   It doesn't mean anything. It's what it's called.

ANTHONY.   Let's go there.

LESLY.   Anthony. I am not gonna go to Pennsylvania with you. I am not gonna go to New York with you. I am not gonna go to the 7-Eleven with you. *(Pause.)*

ANTHONY.   I didn't ask you to go the 7-Eleven with me.

LESLY.   It was an example. For emphasis. I needed a third thing for emphasis. Can you sit on my suitcase?

ANTHONY.   What?

LESLY.   Can you sit on my suitcase?

ANTHONY.   Can I sit on your suitcase? You're standing there asking me if I can sit on your suitcase? You're standing there callously asking me if I can sit on your suitcase when you know and I know as soon as that suitcase is latched you'll swing it off the bed and carry it downstairs and take you and it out of my life.

LESLY.   The hell with it. *(Lesly takes out a few pieces of clothing so that the lid will close. Anthony picks up one of the articles of clothing and presses it to his nose. She snatches it back.)* Stop smelling my clothes!

ANTHONY.   I will never love another woman. I will go to the desert and love only sand.

LESLY.   Sand? What do you mean you'll love only sand? *(Lesly starts for the door with the suitcase.)*

ANTHONY.   You never go hungry in the desert, Lesly. Do you know why?

LESLY.   Why?

ANTHONY.   Because of the sand which is there.

CROSSFADE

Scene 11

The living room. The morning after. Marty's tie and Jackie's hat are askew, their shoes are off, buttons are undone. Empty wine bottles and dirty glasses are strewn about. Mrs. Pascal picks up the glasses.

JACKIE-O. Don't clean, Mother. Honestly. Don't we have a maid?

MRS. PASCAL. Not anymore.

JACKIE-O. What happened to her?

MRS. PASCAL. She quit when you shot your brother.

JACKIE-O. The Kennedys have a maid. The Kennedys have everything.

MRS. PASCAL. Except for luck.

JACKIE-O. I think they're lucky, they're all dead.

MRS. PASCAL. It's too early in the morning to go all morbid. You'll be sleeping in coffins next and drinking out of skulls.

JACKIE-O. It's been done.

MRS. PASCAL. So has Death.

MARTY. It's been done to Death.

MRS. PASCAL. He speaks.

MARTY. What's for breakfast?

MRS. PASCAL. Croissants. They're in the kitchen. They're filled with something. I forget what.

MARTY. I guess we'll find out.

JACKIE-O. How exciting. Don't you find life to be exciting?

MRS. PASCAL. What's that gun doing there?

JACKIE-O. It's not a gun. It's a camera.

MRS. PASCAL. It is too a gun.

JACKIE-O. It's a camera that looks like a gun.

MRS. PASCAL. Give it to me.

MARTY. It's an empty gun.

MRS. PASCAL. How do you know?

MARTY. I checked.

MRS. PASCAL. What is it doing there?

JACKIE-O. Being gun-like, gun-esque.

MRS. PASCAL. Where did it come from?

JACKIE-O. God.

MARTY. We were taking a trip down memory lane.

MRS. PASCAL. I want it now.

JACKIE-O. I'll put it away.

MRS. PASCAL. Marty.

MARTY. *I'll* put it away. *(Marty exits with gun.)*

JACKIE-O. Mother, you're white as a ghost. You look positively Ibsen-esque.

MRS. PASCAL. If it happens again, they'll put you away. They'll just put you away.

JACKIE-O. Only if someone finds out.

MRS. PASCAL. She must have family somewhere.

JACKIE-O. What?

MRS. PASCAL. Lesly.

JACKIE-O. I'm not going to shoot Lesly!

MRS. PASCAL. Just don't.

JACKIE-O. That's all we need is Marty mooning over some dead girl.

MRS. PASCAL. She's leaving anyway.

JACKIE-O. When?

MRS. PASCAL. This morning.

JACKIE-O. Why?

MRS. PASCAL. I suggested it.

JACKIE-O. And she agreed?

MRS. PASCAL. More or less.

JACKIE-O. Why would she leave?

MRS. PASCAL. Maybe we're not her cup of tea.

JACKIE-O. Is Marty going with her?

MRS. PASCAL. Don't be silly.

JACKIE-O. If he leaves again, I'll implode. I'll just implode.

MRS. PASCAL. He's staying.

JACKIE-O. Where is she now?

MRS. PASCAL. Packing I imagine.

JACKIE-O. She's packing?

MRS. PASCAL.   As we speak.

JACKIE-O.   What if she forgets something?

MRS. PASCAL.   We'll burn it. *(Marty re-enters without gun.)* Is it away?

MARTY.   Yes.

MRS. PASCAL.   Did you hide it?

MARTY.   I put it somewhere.

MRS. PASCAL.   But did you hide it?

MARTY.   Only in the sense that I put it somewhere and no one saw me put it there.

MRS. PASCAL.   If I walked into the room where you put the gun, could I see it?

MARTY.   No.

MRS. PASCAL.   Then it's hidden.

JACKIE-O.   Don't worry Mama, we won't bloody the carpets.

MRS. PASCAL.   Do you actually think I'm worried about my carpets?

JACKIE-O.   Aren't you?

MRS. PASCAL.   A little. I had to steam clean the last time. And there's still a sort of shadow. *(Mrs. Pascal disappears. Lesly enters with a suitcase.)*

JACKIE-O.   My. You're up early. Did you sleep all right?

LESLY.   Why are you wearing that costume?

JACKIE-O.   Everything else was in the wash. There's croissants in the kitchen. No pancakes today I'm afraid.

LESLY.   I have to talk to Marty.

JACKIE-O.   I wonder what about. *(Lesly waits for Jackie-O to leave. She doesn't.)*

LESLY.   *(To Marty.)* You were supposed to sneak into my room last night.

MARTY.   I fell asleep.

LESLY.   Did you?

JACKIE-O.   No. He stayed up.

LESLY.   By yourself?

JACKIE-O.   With me.

MARTY.   The hurricane took the Kennedy's stables. The horses got loose. Secret Servicemen were all over the place. Wearing sunglasses.

52

LESLY.   I didn't hear any horses.

MARTY.   What jumped over the moon, a cow or a horse?

LESLY.   A cow.

MARTY.   Oh. I thought it was a horse.

LESLY.   No. A cow.

MARTY.   What's the rest of it? Silverware was involved I know.
Hey diddle diddle … *(Mrs. Pascal appears, carrying a tray of croissants.)*

MRS. PASCAL.   *(To Lesly.)* Lesly, you're up! I see you're all
packed.

LESLY.   Yes.

MRS. PASCAL.   Can I call you a cab?

LESLY.   I don't need a cab.

MRS. PASCAL.   How are you getting to the train station?

LESLY.   I'm going with Marty.

MRS. PASCAL.   He's going to drive you?

LESLY.   He's coming with me.

MRS. PASCAL.   Oh, I don't think so.

LESLY.   He can decide for himself.

MRS. PASCAL.   To make a decision you need all the facts,
and I don't think Marty has all the facts. *(Anthony enters.)* Ah
Anthony, how did you sleep? Did you sleep all right?

ANTHONY.   What?

MRS. PASCAL.   Lesly, how did you sleep, did you sleep all
right?

LESLY.   *(Guarded.)* Yes thank you.

MRS. PASCAL.   Did Anthony sleep all right?

LESLY.   Why don't you ask him?

MRS. PASCAL.   Marty, why don't you ask your brother how
he slept.

MARTY.   Why?

MRS. PASCAL.   Jackie, why don't you ask your brother how
he slept.

JACKIE-O.   How'd you sleep Marty?

MRS. PASCAL.   Your other brother.

JACKIE-O.   How'd you sleep Anthony?

MARTY.   What's going on?

ANTHONY.   Lesly stayed with me last night. *(Beat.)*

JACKIE-O.   Ah, a quaint Pennsylvania pre-nuptial custom.

MRS. PASCAL.   Well I for one am shocked. *(To Lesly.)* Young lady, what *do* you have to say for yourself? *(Lesly says nothing.)*

JACKIE-O.   She's pleading the fifth.

MRS. PASCAL.   I never cared for that symphony.

JACKIE-O.   Wasn't he deaf by then?

MRS. PASCAL.   Call me old-fashioned but I'd say the wedding's off.

JACKIE-O.   It's just as well. I always cry at weddings.

MRS. PASCAL.   I even cried at mine. I must have had a pre-monition.

MARTY.   Get out.

JACKIE-O.   And go where?

MARTY.   There, I imagine.

JACKIE-O.   I hate to go *there,* I like to be *here.*

MRS. PASCAL.   When you go there, it becomes here.

JACKIE-O.   It does?

MRS. PASCAL.   Come on, I'll show you. *(Mrs. Pascal exits. Jackie-O scoops something off the coffee table and follows.)*

ANTHONY.   If you really cared about her you wouldn't a brought her here.

LESLY.   I wanted to come here.

MARTY.   And you did. Come. Or didn't you?

LESLY.   Don't. *(Beat.)*

ANTHONY.   You don't deserve her. *(Anthony exits.)*

MARTY.   How was he?

LESLY.   I can't tell you.

MARTY.   Weren't you there?

LESLY.   I was there but ...

MARTY.   What?

LESLY.   He didn't want you to know.

MARTY.   I'll bet.

LESLY.   How he was.

MARTY.   That good, huh?

LESLY.   It was his first time.

MARTY.   Yeah. Right.

LESLY.   It wasn't?

MARTY.   What do you think?

LESLY.   Then why would he say it?

MARTY.   To get laid.

LESLY.   Well I'm sorry but when somebody says something I tend to think it's the truth, it's just the way I am, the way I was brought up, and if somebody *forgets* to mention something I wouldn't think to ask for example did you sleep with your sister?! *(Pause.)*

MARTY.   Do you think masturbation counts as infidelity?

LESLY.   What?

MARTY.   When I sleep with me and not you am I cheating on you?

LESLY.   Marty. Stop it. I came downstairs before.

MARTY.   Before when?

LESLY.   During it, the thing.

MARTY.   What thing?

LESLY.   The thing with the gun. And the costume.

MARTY.   Oh God.

LESLY.   Why do you do that? *(Marty doesn't answer.)* Do you want me to leave?

MARTY.   You gotta help me.

LESLY.   How?

MARTY.   Talk me back. Tell me about Sundays. What you and I would do on a Sunday.

LESLY.   We'd get up.

MARTY.   Right. Right. We'd get up. What about the alarm? Did the alarm go off?

LESLY.   No alarm baby, it's Sunday.

MARTY.   Oh. Oh yeah. Sunday.

LESLY.   The digital clock says 10:39. I climb out of bed. I pull the comforter over your bare shoulder. The cat is weaving in and out of my legs.

MARTY.   Coco.

LESLY.   I feed her. I come back to bed. I stroke your cheek. My fingers smell like tuna fish.

MARTY.   I pull you down onto me. You have rings, mascara rings, like a football player.

LESLY.   You have bad breath. I kiss you anyway.

MARTY.   I watch you dress. I feel sad when you buckle your bra. There they go, I think, there they go.

LESLY.   I lose my other shoe.

MARTY.   I find your other shoe.

LESLY.   We read menus in the windows on Avenue A. We read the right side. We go to the Mogador. I forget what Eggs Florentine is.

MARTY.   Like Benedict with spinach.

LESLY.   The waitress says toast or pita? Toast or pita?

MARTY.   What about the newspaper? We forgot to buy a newspaper!

LESLY.   Later, newspaper comes later. We go to a street fair. I buy you a scarf.

MARTY.   Blue.

LESLY.   You buy me a barrette, a barrette with a bone.

MARTY.   Pebbles, like Pebbles.

LESLY.   We buy tulips.

MARTY.   Pink.

LESLY.   And a Sunday *Times.* We go home. It's late afternoon and the sign comes on.

MARTY.   Jesus saves.

LESLY.   Across the street.

MARTY.   Jesu Salva.

LESLY.   We run a bath, you wash my back.

MARTY.   Shoulders like wings, bird shoulders.

LESLY.   Marty I want you to leave with me. I want you to leave with me now.

MARTY.   Yes. All right. Yes. (*A toilet flushes loudly. Jackie-O stands in the doorway.*)

JACKIE-O.   I just flushed your car keys down the toilet.

LESLY.   Marty, gimme your keys.

MARTY.   (*Checking his pockets.*) I don't have them.

LESLY.   Where's your extra set?

MARTY.   In my room.

LESLY.   Get them.

MARTY.   At home.

LESLY.   We'll call a cab. Where's the phone book?

MARTY.   By the phone. (*Lesly goes to the phone table.*)

56

LESLY.   The *yellow* pages.

MARTY.   Underneath.

LESLY.   The phone's dead.

JACKIE-O.   Don't look at me.

LESLY.   Marty's not gonna stay here with you, we're leaving for New York this morning, I don't care how. Anthony told me about you, he told me what you did to that lizard. *(Anthony appears in the doorway.)*

JACKIE-O.   Oh Anthony, not that old lizard story ...

LESLY.   And I know what else you did, I know where the scar came from, I know why they sent you to the hospital.

JACKIE-O.   You're a regular Nancy Drew ...

LESLY.   You're making him crazy, you want him to be crazy like you. Look at yourself, look at your clothes, you're making fun of a woman who lost her husband, a man *died,* a man was *murdered,* a man who did something for other people ... what have you ever done for somebody else? If you really love Marty, think about what his life would be like here in this house, your mother will die, you'll be left alone, you'll have babies with webbed feet that you bury out back in the yard ...

JACKIE-O.   Where in the yard?

LESLY.   What?

JACKIE-O.   Where exactly in the yard? On the croquet lawn? By the bird bath? Marty, where do you think we should bury these babies with webbed feet? The back yard is getting very crowded I think. Positively littered with corpses. First Daddy's and now duck babies.

LESLY.   You killed your father?

JACKIE-O.   Not me. Mama.

MARTY.   My father left my mother. Years ago. The day Kennedy was shot.

JACKIE-O.   He tried to leave but Mama shot him. We buried him by the central air.

MARTY.   They were installing central air, there was a hole in the ground, but not for him, for the air conditioner, she's confused, you're confused Jackie, he left Mama, he called a cab ...

JACKIE-O.   She covered him with her body, she tried to keep him there ...

MARTY.   Jackie Kennedy, not Mama, Jackie Kennedy ...

JACKIE-O.   She tried to keep his head on, but it was falling off ...

MARTY.   Lesly, go get your suitcase. *(Lesly exits.)* Anthony, go with her.

ANTHONY.   Give her her pills, Marty.

MARTY.   Which pills?

ANTHONY.   I don't know which pills, she changed pills. *(Jackie-O pulls out the gun.)*

JACKIE-O.   One more time Marty? For old time's sake?

ANTHONY.   She's got a gun. Get the gun!

MARTY.   It's only blanks.

JACKIE-O.   One more time and I'll give you the car keys.

ANTHONY.   *(Rummaging through prescription bottles.)* Here's the blue ones, try the blue ones.

JACKIE-O.   One more time, that's all I ask, then you can go back to the land of the donut kings ...

ANTHONY.   What does she want? What is she doing?

MARTY.   Anthony, go get Mama.

ANTHONY.   Give her the blue ones, I think it's the blue ones.

MARTY.   Go! *(Anthony exits.)*

JACKIE-O.   You be him.

MARTY.   Yes.

JACKIE-O.   And I'll be her.

MARTY.   I'm him?

JACKIE-O.   And I'm her. *(Jackie-O lifts the gun and points it at him. She shoots. Three spotlights pick up the faces of the other three characters at the moment they hear the gunshot. Marty falls back on the couch. Jackie-O drops the gun and falls beside him cradling his head in her hands. They are both drenched with blood. Their position echoes the position of the Kennedys the moment after the assassination. Mrs. Pascal drops her cocktail glass. Amplified sound of glass shattering. Outside the wind dies.)*

PROPERTY LIST

Cocktail glass with ice (MRS. PASCAL)
Tray of wine glasses with wine (MARTY)
Wet clothing (LESLY)
Ice cube (MARTY)
Clothes (LESLY)
Matches (MARTY)
Candle (ANTHONY)
Shoe with broken heel (LESLY)
Pink pill-box hat (JACKIE-O)
Pink Chanel suit (JACKIE-O)
Gun (JACKIE-O)
Suitcase (LESLY)
Hairbrush (LESLY)
Empty wine bottles
Dirty drinking glasses
Tray of croissants (MRS. PASCAL)
Prescription bottles with pills (MRS. PASCAL)

SOUND EFFECTS

Hurricane
Banging of a window
Ice, in glasses, tinkling; amplified
Toilet flush
Glass shattering, amplified
Wind dying down

NEW PLAYS

★ **A LESSON BEFORE DYING by Romulus Linney, based on the novel by Ernest J. Gaines.** An innocent young man is condemned to death in backwoods Louisiana and must learn to die with dignity. "The story's wrenching power lies not in its outrage but in the almost inexplicable grace the characters must muster as their only resistance to being treated like lesser beings." *—The New Yorker.* "Irresistable momentum and a cathartic explosion…a powerful inevitability." *—NY Times.* [5M, 2W] ISBN: 0-8222-1785-6

★ **BOOM TOWN by Jeff Daniels.** A searing drama mixing small-town love, politics and the consequences of betrayal. "…a brutally honest, contemporary foray into classic themes, exploring what moves people to lie, cheat, love and dream. By BOOM TOWN's climactic end there are no secrets, only bare truth." *—Oakland Press.* "…some of the most electrifying writing Daniels has ever done…" *—Ann Arbor News.* [2M, 1W] ISBN: 0-8222-1760-0

★ **INCORRUPTIBLE by Michael Hollinger.** When a motley order of medieval monks learns their patron saint no longer works miracles, a larcenous, one-eyed minstrel shows them an outrageous new way to pay old debts. "A lightning-fast farce, rich in both verbal and physical humor." *—American Theatre.* "Everything fits snugly in this funny, endearing black comedy…an artful blend of the mock-formal and the anachronistically breezy…A piece of remarkably dexterous craftsmanship." *—Philadelphia Inquirer.* "A farcical romp, scintillating and irreverent." *—Philadelphia Weekly.* [5M, 3W] ISBN: 0-8222-1787-2

★ **CELLINI by John Patrick Shanley.** Chronicles the life of the original "Renaissance Man," Benvenuto Cellini, the sixteenth-century Italian sculptor and man-about-town. Adapted from the autobiography of Benvenuto Cellini, translated by J. Addington Symonds. "[Shanley] has created a convincing Cellini, not neglecting his dark side, and a trim, vigorous, fast-moving show." *—BackStage.* "Very entertaining…With brave purpose, the narrative undermines chronology before untangling it…touching and funny…" *—NY Times.* [7M, 2W (doubling)] ISBN: 0-8222-1808-9

★ **PRAYING FOR RAIN by Robert Vaughan.** Examines a burst of fatal violence and its aftermath in a suburban high school. "Thought provoking and compelling." *—Denver Post.* "Vaughan's powerful drama offers hope and possibilities." *—Theatre.com.* "[The play] doesn't put forth compact, tidy answers to the problem of youth violence. What it does offer is a compelling exploration of the forces that influence an individual's choices, and of the proverbial lifelines—be they familial, communal, religious or political—that tragically slacken when society gives in to apathy, fear and self-doubt…" *—Westword.* "…a symphony of anger…" *—Gazette Telegraph.* [4M, 3W] ISBN: 0-8222-1807-0

★ **GOD'S MAN IN TEXAS by David Rambo.** When a young pastor takes over one of the most prestigious Baptist churches from a rip-roaring old preacher-entrepreneur, all hell breaks loose. "…the pick of the litter of all the works at the Humana Festival…" *—Providence Journal.* "…a wealth of both drama and comedy in the struggle for power…" *—LA Times.* "…the first act is so funny…deepens in the second act into a sobering portrait of fear, hope and self-delusion…" *—Columbus Dispatch.* [3M] ISBN: 0-8222-1801-1

★ **JESUS HOPPED THE 'A' TRAIN by Stephen Adly Guirgis.** A probing, intense portrait of lives behind bars at Rikers Island. "…fire-breathing…whenever it appears that JESUS is settling into familiar territory, it slides right beneath expectations into another, fresher direction. It has the courage of its intellectual restlessness…[JESUS HOPPED THE 'A' TRAIN] has been written in flame." *—NY Times.* [4M, 1W] ISBN: 0-8222-1799-6

DRAMATISTS PLAY SERVICE, INC.
440 Park Avenue South, New York, NY 10016 212-683-8960 Fax 212-213-1539
postmaster@dramatists.com www.dramatists.com

NEW PLAYS

★ **THE CIDER HOUSE RULES, PARTS 1 & 2 by Peter Parnell, adapted from the novel by John Irving.** Spanning eight decades of American life, this adaptation from the Irving novel tells the story of Dr. Wilbur Larch, founder of the St. Cloud's, Maine orphanage and hospital, and of the complex father-son relationship he develops with the young orphan Homer Wells. "...luxurious digressions, confident pacing...an enterprise of scope and vigor..." –NY Times. "...The fact that I can't wait to see Part 2 only begins to suggest just how good it is..." –NY Daily News. "...engrossing...an odyssey that has only one major shortcoming: It comes to an end." –Seattle Times. "...outstanding...captures the humor, the humility...of Irving's 588-page novel..." –Seattle Post-Intelligencer. [9M, 10W, doubling, flexible casting] PART 1 ISBN: 0-8222-1725-2 PART 2 ISBN: 0-8222-1726-0

★ **TEN UNKNOWNS by Jon Robin Baitz.** An iconoclastic American painter in his seventies has his life turned upside down by an art dealer and his ex-boyfriend. "...breadth and complexity...a sweet and delicate harmony rises from the four cast members...Mr. Baitz is without peer among his contemporaries in creating dialogue that spontaneously conveys a character's social context and moral limitations..." –NY Times. "...darkly funny, brilliantly desperate comedy...TEN UNKNOWNS vibrates with vital voices." –NY Post. [3M, 1W] ISBN: 0-8222-1826-7

★ **BOOK OF DAYS by Lanford Wilson.** A small-town actress playing St. Joan struggles to expose a murder. "...[Wilson's] best work since Fifth of July...An intriguing, prismatic and thoroughly engrossing depiction of contemporary small-town life with a murder mystery at its core...a splendid evening of theater..." –Variety. "...fascinating...a densely populated, unpredictable little world." –St. Louis Post-Dispatch. [6M, 5W] ISBN: 0-8222-1767-8

★ **THE SYRINGA TREE by Pamela Gien.** Winner of the 2001 Obie Award. A breathtakingly beautiful tale of growing up white in apartheid South Africa. "Instantly engaging, exotic, complex, deeply shocking...a thoroughly persuasive transport to a time and a place...stun[s] with the power of a gut punch..." –NY Times. "Astonishing...affecting ...[with] a dramatic and heartbreaking conclusion...A deceptive sweet simplicity haunts THE SYRINGA TREE..." –A.P. [1W (or flexible cast)] ISBN: 0-8222-1792-9

★ **COYOTE ON A FENCE by Bruce Graham.** An emotionally riveting look at capital punishment. "The language is as precise as it is profane, provoking both troubling thought and the occasional cheerful laugh...will change you a little before it lets go of you." –Cincinnati CityBeat. "...excellent theater in every way..." –Philadelphia City Paper. [3M, 1W] ISBN: 0-8222-1738-4

★ **THE PLAY ABOUT THE BABY by Edward Albee.** Concerns a young couple who have just had a baby and the strange turn of events that transpire when they are visited by an older man and woman. "An invaluable self-portrait of sorts from one of the few genuinely great living American dramatists...rockets into that special corner of theater heaven where words shoot off like fireworks into dazzling patterns and hues." –NY Times. "An exhilarating, wicked...emotional terrorism." –NY Newsday. [2M, 2W] ISBN: 0-8222-1814-3

★ **FORCE CONTINUUM by Kia Corthron.** Tensions among black and white police officers and the neighborhoods they serve form the backdrop of this discomfiting look at life in the inner city. "The creator of this intense...new play is a singular voice among American playwrights...exceptionally eloquent..." –NY Times. "...a rich subject and a wise attitude." –NY Post. [6M, 2W, 1 boy] ISBN: 0-8222-1817-8

DRAMATISTS PLAY SERVICE, INC.
440 Park Avenue South, New York, NY 10016 212-683-8960 Fax 212-213-1539
postmaster@dramatists.com   www.dramatists.com